AN ALBUM OF MOTORCYCLES AND MOTORCYCLE RACING

AN ALBUM OF MOTORCYCLES AND MOTORCYCLE RACING

BY ELWOOD D. BAUMANN

FRANKLIN WATTS
New York • London • Toronto • Sydney
1982

Cover photographs courtesy of Daytona International Speedway Corp.: (top, left and right); Imperial War Museum: (bottom).

Photographs courtesy of: The Science Museum, London, England: pp. 2 (top), 6 (top), 10 (bottom), 11 (bottom), 14 (bottom), 22 (bottom); National Motor Museum: pp. 3 (top), 5 (both), 6 (bottom), 8, 10 (top), 11 (top), 12 (both), 14 (top), 15 (both), 16 (both), 17 (both), 24, 25 (both), 26 (all), 27, 66 (both), 67 (both), 68 (bottom); Smithsonian Institution: pp. 2 (bottom); 3 (bottom); Harley Davidson Motor Co., Inc.: pp. 19, 20 (both), 21 (both), 22 (top), 35, 76 (bottom), 78 (both), 79; Imperial War Museum: 28, 29 (both); United Press International: pp. 32 (top), 74; Wembley Stadium Ltd.: p. 32 (bottom); Daytona International Speedway Corp.: pp. 33, 38 (bottom), 40, 41 (both), 42 (both), 43, 44, 45, 46, 47 (bottom), 49, 50 (top), 54, 55, 56, 57, 58, 59 (both), 60, 61 (both), 62, 63 (all); American Motorcycle Association: p. 34; David M. Doody: p. 37; Goodyear Tire Co.: p. 38 (top); U.S. Suzuki Motor Corp: pp. 47 (top), 69 (both); News-Journal Corp., Daytona, Florida: 50 (bottom by Pete Wright), 51 (by Pam Leckeby), 52 (by Roger Simms), 53 (both by Elizabeth Reed); American Honda Motor Co.: pp. 68 (top), 75; Roy W. Pratt: pp. 70, 71; Yamaha: p. 76 (top); BMW: p. 77.

Library of Congress Cataloging in Publication Data

Baumann, Elwood D.
An album of motorcycles and motorcycle racing.

Bibliography: p.
Includes index.
Summary: Text and photographs discuss early models of motorcycles and the first races, the development of big motorcycle companies, the evolution of motorcycle sports, and the popularity of scooters and mopeds.
1. Motorcycle racing—Juvenile literature.
2. Motorcycles—Juvenile literature.
[1. Motorcycles.   2. Motorcycle—racing]   I. Title.
GV1060.B34   1982 796.7'5 82-8427
ISBN 0-531-04469-6   AACR2

CONTENTS

AN ALBUM OF MOTORCYCLES AND MOTORCYCLE RACING

1 SOMETHING NEW ON THE ROADS

A GERMAN INVENTS A VERY STRANGE MACHINE

Gottlieb Daimler was very pleased with the single-cylinder internal-combustion engine he had just finished building. There was only one problem: He wasn't exactly sure what practical purpose it would serve.

Daimler was still trying to figure out how his invention could be used when his son, Paul, came into the workshop. Paul was tired. He had just pedaled his bicycle home from Cannstatt, Germany, and it had been uphill all the way.

Suddenly, Gottlieb Daimler had an idea. He would build a bicycle, and it would be powered by his new gasoline engine. He went to work at once. The machine was finished on the morning of November 10, 1885. That afternoon Paul Daimler rode it from Cannstatt to Unterturkheim and back, a journey of about seven miles (12 km).

It was quite a ride! The ungainly, top-heavy vehicle bounced over holes, ruts, and rocks. The engine bellowed. A trail of smoke poured from the machine, looking as though it was coming from the seat of Paul's trousers. Onlookers stared in amazement as Paul roared slowly past. Nearly every dog between Cannstatt and Unterturkheim tried to take a bite out of his leg. Paul, however, wasn't worried about the dogs. He was too busy trying to keep his "motorcycle" in an upright position.

AMERICA'S FIRST MOTORCYCLE

The steam-powered, three-wheeled motorcycle—invented by Sylvester H. Roper of Roxbury, Massachusetts, around 1869—could boast neither speed nor beauty. Roper, however, was enormously proud of his creation, which he called a velocipede, and told everyone that it was a mechanical marvel. His motorcycle was probably the first one seen on the American continent.

Roper's invention became quite a common sight in New England. He toured as many fairs and circuses as possible and declared that he was willing to race any horse in the area. The locals all agreed that Roper's steam buggy was very interesting, but they couldn't imagine what good it would ever do anyone.

THERE AIN'T NOTHIN' LIKE A HORSE

The motorcycle invented in 1884 by Lucius D. Copeland of Philadelphia was actually better than it looked. The front wheel was very much larger than the back one. It was powered by a lightweight

Above: this forerunner of the motorcycle was invented in France in 1818. It was called the Velocipe-draisiavaporianna! *Right:* Roper's steam velocipede was not the only one in the world, despite his boasting. Several European countries already had similar machines on the road.

THE GREATEST
MECHANICAL
EXHIBITION
IN THE WORLD.

THE
STEAM
BUGGY!

Pronounced by scientific men to be the most wonderful invention of modern times. It can be driven, with two persons in it, 150 miles a day, upon common roads. It is light and strong, and can be managed better than any horse, and can be driven faster than any person dare to ride. Will match it against any trotting horse in the world.

THE ONLY
Steam Velocipede
IN THE WORLD.

Pronounced a perfect triumph in mechanism. It can be driven up any hill, and will out speed any horse in the world.

TO BE SEEN AT
600 BROADWAY.

Left: many feel that this German invention is the world's first motorcycle. The exact date that this was made is unknown. *Below:* Sylvester Roper decided that two-wheeled vehicles, like this one, were impractical, so he went on to invent three- and four-wheeled vehicles.

steam engine which drove a complicated array of pulleys and belts. The driver had to perch on top of the front wheel and was kept busy manipulating an assortment of gadgets that controlled the flow of steam. While doing all this, the driver also had to steer and maintain his balance.

There seemed to be no limit to Copeland's enterprise. His next invention was a three-wheeler, called the Phaeton Moto-Cycle. Two passengers sat in the front and the driver sat in the back. The machine could travel for 30 miles (48 km) at a speed of 10 miles (16 km) per hour, but Copeland still wasn't satisfied.

In 1887, Copeland formed the Northrop Manufacturing Company of Camden, New Jersey, which produced reliable Phaeton Moto-Cycles.

In 1888, Copeland began producing a steam-powered motor-cycle built for two. The inventor later added a third wheel on the side of this motorcycle so that it wouldn't tip over when standing motion-less, and a seat for a third passenger. In later years, this conveyance came to be known as the sidecar.

Unfortunately, the Northrop Manufacturing Company was not a success. One of the reasons for its failure is quite simple. A local paper reported that a farmer who had studied the contraption in the showroom for a few seconds said: "There ain't nothin' like a horse." He then sniffed disdainfully before stalking off.

PROBLEMS IN ENGLAND

At a time when America, France, Germany, and a number of other countries were building a car and motorcycle industry, nothing seemed to be happening in England.

This was a peculiar situation. England was the home of mechanical enterprise. Why, then, wasn't the country taking more of an interest in the new motor-carriage industry?

The answer was surprisingly simple. The Locomotives on Highways Acts of 1861 and 1865 had destroyed virtually all mechanical initiative.

The law declared that every engine-powered vehicle traveling on even the remotest country road had to have two able-bodied men in attendance. A third man had to walk in front of the vehicle. During the day, he had to carry a red warning flag. At night, he had to switch to a red lamp. It was also his duty to see that the vehicles never exceeded a speed of 4 miles (6 km) per hour!

Such high speeds could not be maintained in towns or villages. The maximum speed allowed in populated areas was 2 miles (3 km) per hour.

It was not until 1896 that the law prohibiting speeds in excess of 4 miles per hour was taken off the books.

THE ELECTRIC SPEED DEMON

In 1898, the Humber Company exhibited an electric tandem at London's Stanley Show. Its neat appearance and simple design made a

Left: Lucius D. Copeland was the only person able to ride his two-wheeled steam motorcycle—and even he fell off occasionally. *Below:* explosions were not uncommon on this early British tricycle built for two—and the steam tank was directly beneath the driver's seat!

Right: Ernest Michaux's "Boneshaker." *Below:* some historians regard Edward Butler's gasoline-burning tricycle as the world's first motorcycle.

very favorable impression on the crowd. The power plant was simply a series of storage batteries connected to the motor.

There were many good points about the electric tandem. Unlike other vehicles, which made an earsplitting racket, Humber's invention was virtually silent. It was also easy to ride, capable of high speeds, and required no cranking.

The vehicle, however, did have one rather serious shortcoming: It could run only as long as the battery cells were charged, and that, unfortunately, was not very long.

Today there is renewed interest in vehicles powered by electricity. Oil and gas may soon be in short supply, but the world has all the electricity it needs.

So who knows? The electric motorcycle may turn out to be the vehicle of the future.

A FRENCHMAN BRINGS HIS MOTORCYCLE TO ENGLAND

In the summer of 1868, Ernest Michaux brought his bicycle with a front wheel pedal to England. Several French companies were already manufacturing the machines, and the Frenchman thought that Britain might be a good market. This "Boneshaker," as it was called, was an ancestor of the modern bicycle and motorcycle.

Michaux's machine had no springs, so riders had to hang on tightly as the high wheels bounced over ruts and rocks.

Riding the "Boneshaker" was a problem. And stopping it was an even tougher proposition! This was accomplished by pushing the handlebars forward, which tightened a cord attached to a block of wood in the rear. The wood pressed against the back tire, slowing down the motorcycle. When the "Boneshaker" had come to an almost complete halt, the rider jumped off and hoped for the best.

Ernest Michaux's machine was of great interest to the British inventors. It moved slowly and noisily, but it did move. With a little effort, they hoped to build a much better "boneshaker."

THE PETROL-CYCLE

Who invented the world's first motorcycle? Some historians say that is was Gottlieb Daimler. Others insist that it was a shy, quiet Englishman named Edward Butler. Luckily, Butler was not too shy to display his gasoline-burning tricycle at the Inventors' Exhibition in London in 1885. The unusual machine attracted quite a bit of attention.

Over the years, Butler made many improvements on his machine, which he called a petrol-cycle. Unfortunately, as the petrol-cycle got better and better, the inventor's financial position got worse and worse.

The speed limit in Britain was still 4 miles (6 km) per hour in the country and 2 miles (3 km) an hour in town. People just wouldn't buy a machine that could move no faster than they could walk!

Butler stopped working on his beloved petrol-cycle in 1896, and the general belief is that it was broken up for scrap. No trace of it ever appeared anywhere.

EDWARD J. PENNINGTON —GYP OR GENIUS?

It seems that Edward J. Pennington was really not much of an inventor. Among his many failures were airships that never got into the air and propeller-assisted bicycles that could go no faster than any other kind of bicycle.

Motorcycling was catching on fast in Europe, so Pennington built one and sailed for England from America. He immediately launched a gigantic publicity campaign. He told the public that his motorcycle could speed along easily at 65 miles (104 km) an hour. Not only that, but it could also jump rivers!

Pennington must have been one of the greatest salespeople of all times. After a lot of fast talking, he managed to sell the British rights to his motorcycle to a patent speculator named H. J. Lawson. The price was a staggering half million dollars.

The Great Horseless Carriage Company was doomed from the very beginning. Pennington's designs were useless, but Lawson believed in his genius.

This was a fatal mistake. The money was soon gone, and the Great Horseless Carriage Company went broke in 1899.

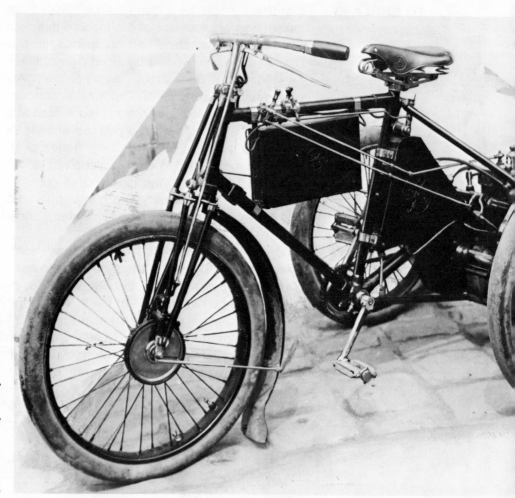

An adventurer tried to go around the world in one of these 1898 De Dion tricycles from Britain. However, he broke down just 10 miles (16 km) from home.

2 THE BIRTH OF COMPETITION

RUNS AND RACES

Although not everyone agrees, the first motorcycle race was probably run in France in 1896. It was sponsored by the Automobile Club of Paris and went from Paris to Nantes and back. This was a total distance of 95 miles (152 km). Nobody really knows who won the race because there were no finishers!

The British finally repealed the Locomotives on Highways Acts in 1896. Vehicles could now rip along at any speed up to 12 miles (19 km) per hour. To celebrate, it was decided to hold a 52-mile (83-km) run from London to Brighton. The run began at sunup and anyone who arrived at the destination by nightfall would be considered a winner. Night, however, fell well before the first vehicle came roaring down the road.

Eighteen ninety-six was a banner year for motorcycling. The first race and the first run in history were both held that year. (A race is run for speed on a set or closed course; a run usually refers to another form of competition, such as an enduro or observed trial.)

PROBLEM NUMBER ONE —GETTING IT STARTED

Some manufacturers lamented the fact that so few women drove motorcycles. There was, however, a perfectly good reason for this. In many cases, it took tremendous strength and stamina to get a motorcycle going. Pushing a motorcycle block after block to get it started was exhausting.

Cold weather was also a problem. It was usually necessary for the cyclist to put the rear wheel up on a stand, then pedal like mad until the engine oil became somewhat less coarse and heavy.

An engine that hadn't been started for several days always proved to be a problem. It often came to life just seconds before the owner fell flat on his face from sheer exhaustion. In many cases, the engine sputtered and coughed only until the owner crawled weakly onto the saddle. Then it again fell dead and silent. By this time, the owner probably felt like doing the same.

The lucky owners were those who lived on the top of a very long hill. The long ride down was usually enough to urge even the coldest engine into life. If that didn't work, though, the owner had to start the long push back up to the top and try again.

Many improvements have been made on motorcycles over the years, but the invention of the kick starter must certainly rank as the

Right: before racing was permitted on public roads in England, cyclists raced across fields and through forests. *Below:* the Wolf-müller "motor bicycle" of 1894 had rubber tires, which were considered revolutionary at the time.

Left: racers in trouble could always count on helping hands. *Below:* the Werner steam motorcycle of 1899, although ahead of its time, ran out of steam after short distances.

Above: the Isle of Man Tourist Trophy is regarded by some as the toughest, most dangerous race in the world. *Right:* Kaye Donne, one of Britain's first motorcycle racing heroes, at Brooklands Race Track around 1920.

greatest improvement of them all. It was now no longer necessary to run and jump on to get a cycle going.

Today, electric starters make revving up motorcycles simple.

UPHILL AND DOWNHILL

Hills were nightmares for the early motorcyclists. Coming down was just as bad as going up.

Fuel flow was the big problem in hill climbing. Gas had to flow from the tank (in the back of the motorcycle) up front to the engine. Water cannot flow uphill, and the same thing is true of gasoline. If the hill was too steep, the gas could not reach the engine. The engine then died of fuel starvation, and the driver had to get off and push.

The driver's troubles were far from over when he reached the top of the hill. Going down the other side was a terrifying experience. The brakes were very primitive affairs that often failed. The driver often ended up tearing helplessly down a hill at top speed.

THE ISLE OF MAN TOURIST TROPHY

Racing was not a popular sport in Britain at the turn of the century, because the authorities refused to let cyclists race on public roads. But then cyclists were invited to the Isle of Man, off the west coast of England. They were not only free to race over the island's roads, but they would have the roads all to themselves during the race.

The Isle of Man is 227 square miles (588 sq. km) of very hilly countryside in the Irish Sea. The course, known as the Mountain Circuit, is 38 miles (60 km) long. There are 264 curves and corners on the narrow road, and any one of them could spell disaster. All motorcyclists agree that the Isle of Man is the toughest, most exciting, and most dangerous motorcycle race in the world. It is so dangerous, in fact, that many of the top drivers refuse to race there.

Motorcycle races have been run on the island annually since 1907 except during the war years. There can be no doubt that the Isle of Man Tourist Trophy is the world's most famous motorcycling event. It has enjoyed tremendous public support for over 70 years and is becoming more popular all the time.

"If the crowds get any larger," said one of the locals, "they'll probably sink the whole island and we'll all wind up in China."

MOTORCYCLING —SPORT AND PASTIME

Women and elderly people gradually became interested in motorcycling as a sport and pastime. Manufacturers were told exactly what the new enthusiasts wanted: a lightweight motorcycle that made a minimum amount of noise. It had to have at least two gears and be capable of cruising at 20 miles (32 km) per hour without vibrating. Above all, it had to be easy to start.

The new enthusiasts meant thousands of additional sales, and the manufacturers turned eagerly to their drawing boards. By 1955, over a dozen British companies were producing well-designed middleweight motorcycles, and by 1962, the Japanese were producing a lightweight Honda model.

Left: cyclists loved Britain's Triumph Motorcycle of 1915, even though sparks flew from it and the gas tank was underneath the driver's body. *Below:* the J.D. motorcycle was popular in England just after World War I.

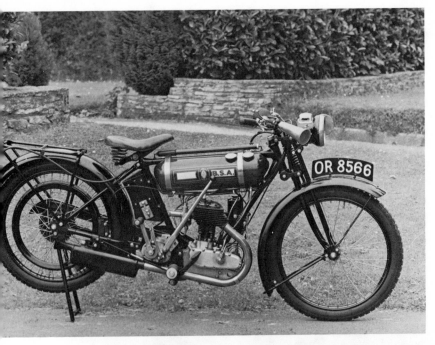

Left: England's B.S.A. of 1925 was noted for speed and comfort. *Below:* this 1931 British Matchless is over fifty years old, but it looks very much like motor-cycles on the roads today.

Early motorcycle advertisements

3 THE BIG COMPANIES MAKE THE SCENE

HARLEY-DAVIDSON, GREATEST OF THEM ALL

William Harley, a draftsman, and Arthur Davidson, a pattern maker, were a fortunate team. Both were amateur inventors whose main interest was motorcycles. They were men of vision who made Harley-Davidson the greatest name in American motorcycle production.

When their first motorcycle factory was opened, engine parts were nonexistent. The first carburetor, for example, was fashioned from an old tomato soup can! The two men had to experiment and improvise every inch of the way, but by 1903 they finally had a motorcycle that they were sure would run.

A small crowd was on hand that warm spring afternoon in 1903 when Harley appeared at the door of the factory with their first motorcycle.

He ran alongside as he pushed it around in a circle. Then he hopped on and began pedaling furiously. After a few seconds, the engine roared to life and Harley gave a roar of triumph.

The crowd cheered madly as the inventor rode proudly round and round the factory. The machine did not go very fast, but Harley wasn't perturbed. That was a minor matter that could be worked on later. The important thing was that the motorcycle was a success.

The Harley-Davidson, in fact, became a howling success. Many fans believed that it was the finest motorcycle in existence. That's exactly what Harley and Davidson wanted people to think, and they never stopped trying to improve their product.

In 1908, Harley and Davidson entered the field of sporting competition. For the next few years, their special racing motorcycles carried off one prize after another.

All that, however, came to an end when the United States entered World War I. The Army ordered 20,000 Harley-Davidsons, and racing was forgotten.

That, however, was only temporary. The war ended, and racing resumed almost immediately thereafter. Harley-Davidsons once again began to win many of the races, and they're still doing the same today.

A CHAMPION NAMED CHAMPION

Speed became more and more important all the time. Then, as now, there was always someone who wanted to be the fastest man in the world. One of those men was Albert Champion.

**William Harley and
Arthur Davidson
(in the sidecar)**

Above: the Harley-Davidson factory in 1903. Today, the factory covers a vast area of ground in downtown Milwaukee. *Right:* an American solider on a Harley-Davidson enters Germany at the end of World War I.

Above: this ingenious man
from Wisconsin turned his
Harley-Davidson into a
skimobile. *Right:* part of
an armored division of
Harley-Davidsons during
World War II.

Above: the 1982 FXRS Super Glide II from Harley-Davidson. *Left:* the Indian motorcycle, an American invention, was for a time one of the most popular bikes in the world.

Champion was a French racer and mechanic. Successful racers earned more money in the United States than they did in Europe, so Champion came to the country where the big money was.

It didn't take the Frenchman long at all to make a name for himself. In 1902, he raced around a 1-mile (1.6-km) circular track in just 1 minute and 10 seconds. For a few short months, Champion was the world's speed champion.

Strangely enough, Champion is not remembered because he was a champion. He is remembered more for a spark plug he invented. The AC Spark Plug Division of General Motors actually stands for the Albert Champion Spark Plug Division. Millions of these spark plugs are sold every year.

THE INDIANS ARE COMING! THE INDIANS ARE COMING!

The Indian Company was founded in 1901 and got off to a good start. George Hendee, a bicycle manufacturer, had been eyeing the growing motorcycle market for some time. Oscar Hedstrom, a racer and inventor, felt that he was getting a bit too old for motorcycle racing and was looking around for something else. The two men met at a race one cold February afternoon, and the Indian Company was a result of the meeting.

Success came almost immediately. A racer himself, Hedstrom knew exactly what he wanted. His motorcycles became big sellers almost overnight. Many cyclists said that the Indians were the best motorcycles ever built.

The Indian Company reached the peak of its popularity in 1913. Its main plant in Springfield, Massachusetts, was a building five stories high and three blocks long. Four hundred Indians a day rolled off the assembly line.

During World War I, thousands of bikes were ordered by the military. The famous Indian Scout model became popular in the late 1920s.

The hard times that followed World War II were the beginning of the end.

In 1951 the company was sold to Brockhouse Ltd., in England and renamed the Indian Sales Corporation. Production costs were lower there, and it was hoped that cheaper motorcycles might save the company and keep the name alive.

However, the company folded in 1953. This was incredibly bad luck. The motorcycle boom was about ready to take off and people now had enough money to buy them. Just a few short years would have made a world of difference.

The name of Indian, however, still lives on. A company in California makes minicycles, and another one in Michigan manufactures motorcycles bearing the name of Indian.

They may be Indians, all right, but they don't belong to the same tribe of Indians that were made famous by Oscar Hedstrom and George Hendee. Those Indians were in a class by themselves.

4 PASSENGERS: WELCOME ABOARD

PASSENGERS ARE MOVED FROM BACK TO FRONT

Early in the twentieth century, a few companies began to produce motorcycles with passenger seats.

The first passengers, most of whom were women, were not at all happy with their new means of transportation. They were pulled along in little trailers, and this had certain disadvantages. Dust choked them, the fumes from the motorcycle fuel made them ill, and filthy engine oil splattered them.

A British inventor got the passengers out of the dust, fumes, and filth by building a little seat for them directly behind the driver. They simply had to hang on to the driver and away they went.

This invention was less than ideal. The roads were awful, and the driver often had to swerve sharply and suddenly to miss rocks and holes. This, of course, threw the passenger off balance. Both passenger and driver frequently fell off and lay sprawled in the dirt!

Left: a family in their 1899 De Dion. *Above:* many tricycles, like this 1901 Singer, had a seat behind. *Right:* the Humber Forecar, which put the passenger up front, was an immediate, but brief, sensation.

Above, left: by 1910, Humber and a number of other companies had switched from the forecar to the sidecar, which is still used frequently today. *Above, right:* this double sidecar was used as a promotional gimmick. *Left:* sidecars soon became popular as delivery vehicles. *Right:* the Triumph Company made this torpedo-shaped sidecar in 1912.

SIDECARS Then along came the sidecar. The sidecar was first patented by W.G. Graham in 1903. It was put on the market the same year by the Mills & Fulford Company and became an overnight sensation. Passengers were much happier in a sidecar than they had been on their uncomfortable and unstable little seats in the back.

Every manufacturer tried to have the most handsome and comfortable sidecar on the market. Purchasers had a wide variety of really attractive models to choose from. They came in all designs and colors. Many offered full protection against the weather, and every passenger comfort was considered. Some had luxuriously upholstered reclining seats and virtually all of them had foot warmers.

At long last, the passengers could travel in true style.

Opposite page: an English girl helps a soldier on maneuvers study his map. *Above:* British soldiers in France man machine guns mounted on motorcycles in World War II. Patrols such as these inflicted a great deal of damage because of their high maneuverability. *Left:* dispatch riders stop for a break in the shade of a French farm building.

5 NEW MOTORCYCLE SPORTS

MOTORDROME MADNESS

The first motorcycle board-racing track was built in New Jersey. The sport became so popular that every large city in the United States soon had its own motordrome. Spectacular competitions were held and were always well attended.

Board racing was a very dangerous sport. It was so dangerous, in fact, that many people referred to motordromes as "murder-dromes." The oval tracks were usually about a quarter of a mile (.4 km) long. All of them were steeply banked on the bends to encourage high speeds.

Although the track surface was smooth, it could not be *too* smooth or the motorcycle tires would be unable to get any traction. Anyone who went into a skid at 90 miles (144 km) per hour was in big trouble. If he didn't get badly banged up in the fall, he could be hit by one of the other motorcycles.

Sometimes, the boards became rotten and split wide open. More often, they became saturated with used engine oil. A driver who hit an oil slick would be very lucky indeed if he didn't take a fall.

The small tracks were actually the big problem. Tremendous speeds, the centrifugal pull on the bends, carelessness, oil slicks, and broken boards sent many drivers out of control. Injuries had reached such proportions by 1913 that the authorities called a halt to "motordrome madness."

The sport continued, but on a different scale. Larger and safer board tracks were built. Many of them were 1 and 2 miles (2 and 3 km) in circumference. Higher speeds were possible on the longer tracks, and many records were broken.

TRIALS OF TOUGHNESS

The early motorcyclists were forever telling one another how rugged their machines were. They had to prove it, of course, and nothing was too tough to try. Trials of toughness and reliability were arranged by local clubs.

The Scottish Six Day was by far the most famous. It covered 400 miles (640 km) of murderous terrain. The course bounced over cart tracks and far more often bounced across country where there were no tracks at all. It was usually up one steep hill and down another. The weather in the Scottish Highlands can be terrible, and the cyclists usually had to contend with either snow or rain.

Speed didn't really count for much in the Scottish Six Day. Driving skill and endurance were more important. This wasn't the case, though, in South Africa's Durban to Johannesburg Race. Speed as well as ruggedness and reliability were what counted in this trial.

The Durban to Johannesburg Race was first held in 1913 and was ranked as the longest and most strenuous speed trial in the world. It covered over 400 miles (640 km) of rugged mountain country and was the supreme test for both drivers and machines.

Only the toughest made it all the way.

STUNT RIDING

Nearly everyone has watched stunt riding on television. Some riders shoot through flaming tunnels of fire; others jump over cars and buses. As far back as 1923, South African rider Piet Lievaart held the world motorcycle long-jump record. It was then 62 feet (19 m). The world record for motorcycle jumping is now 195 feet (59 m) and is claimed by Alain Prieur of France. It is also claimed by England's Eddie Kidd.

Although Prieur and Kidd claim to hold the record, Evel Knievel of the United States is a far more famous stuntperson. He once claimed to hold the world record himself, but he declared that jumping over rows of trucks and buses bored him. He wanted to do something more exciting, so he decided to jump across the Grand Canyon on his motorcycle.

The Grand Canyon National Park authorities were astonished when they heard Knievel's plan. The man must be mad, they told one another. No man in his right mind would even consider a stunt like that. Knievel was told in no uncertain terms that he would be arrested on the spot if he tried anything foolish.

The stunt rider was disappointed, but he already had another location in mind. This was the Snake River Canyon, near Twin Falls, Idaho. The canyon was on private land and Knievel leased his launching site from Tom Qualls, the owner.

Knievel was quite pleased with his new location. The Snake River Canyon where he planned to jump was just under a mile (2 km) wide. Six hundred feet (113 m) below the canyon's rim, the river roared and frothed at a tremendous rate. Evel Knievel tried hard to laugh off any worries he might have had. He cheerfully told the crowd that his motorcycle had at least a 50–50 chance of making it. Very few people believed that, but they didn't say so.

Knievel insisted upon calling his vehicle a motorcycle, but it was like no other motorcycle on earth. If everything went right, a rocket would send him soaring across the canyon. If he saw that he wasn't going to make it, he could release a parachute which would lower him to the bottom of the canyon.

Our hero didn't make it. Something went wrong, and the parachute opened as he was shot off the ramp. He dropped down between the canyon walls and was soon rescued by a helicopter.

Right: Evel Knievel attempts to jump across the Snake River Canyon in Idaho— but his rocket ship heads straight down instead. *Below:* before retirement, Evel Knievel was the world's greatest motorcycle stunt-person. *Opposite page:* Doug Domokos, America's Wheelie King, often circles the Daytona Speedway on his rear wheel only. He uses just one hand and one foot to control his bike.

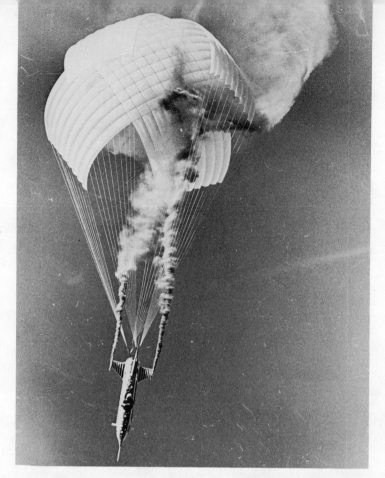

There was no reason for Knievel to be upset over the fact that he hadn't made it to the other side of the Snake River Canyon. His brave attempt had earned him six million dollars.

And that's not bad for an afternoon's work.

THE INTERNATIONAL SIX DAYS ENDURO

This event has been called "the Olympics of Motorcycling," and the term is an apt one. First held in 1917, it is one of the toughest tests of motorcycles and the men who ride them. The run covers from 200 to 250 miles (320 to 400 km) a day. Very little of it is over pavement, much of it is not even over good secondary roads, and much is over unmarked terrain.

At first, the basic requirement was to cross different types of countryside while keeping up an average minimum speed. An all-out speed test was held at the finish of the trial on the sixth day.

This, however, proved unsatisfactory. In 1960, the all-out speed test was abandoned. It was replaced by a series of special tests, which included cross-country speed tests, hill climbs, and observed trials competitions.

Left: the International Six Days Enduro is one of the toughest tests of motorcycles and drivers. *Right:* a cyclist loses his Harley-Davidson in midair.

6 AND MAY THE BEST DRIVER WIN

THE GRAND PRIX RACES

All in all, there are about 50 grand prix races each year. The overwhelming majority of them take place in Europe and the United States. The number varies from year to year, and no one knows until the beginning of the season how many races will be held or where they will be run.

Grand prix racing is truly international in scope. The Belgians, French, Dutch, Spanish, Italians, Germans, Swiss, and a few other European countries have their annual events. Russia also participates. Russian naval motorcycles are present at all events. The Czechoslovakian CZs are also popular and well-constructed machines.

Oddly enough, little Belgium has produced more than its share of champions. This may be because the Spa-Francorchamps Circuit near Spa, Belgium, is the fastest road circuit of them all. It's interesting to note, though, that winners of the Belgian Grand Prix are seldom locals. It seems that Belgians simply cannot win on their home ground.

This may possibly explain why only Dutch riders were permitted to compete in the early Dutch motorcycle grand prix. We can't regard this as a sporting proposition, but it was at least a guarantee that a Dutch driver would win the event.

SAND RACING

Sand racing became very popular in England during the 1920s. Local clubs grabbed nearly every decent stretch of beach for their meets, and the events were usually well attended.

The experts had a rather unique way of riding. To cut down on wind resistance, they leaned as far forward as possible. Many even removed the seats from their motorcycles and put a small cushion in its place. It was a very uncomfortable way to travel, but winning the race was the important thing.

Spectators preferred the longer races of 25 or 50 miles (40 or 80 km). The course was usually oval-shaped, with one edge of the oval running alongside the beach. Marker flags in the sand formed the boundaries of the course.

It was always full throttle all the way. Racers roared around and around the circuit, trying to squeeze the last tiny bit of speed and power from their machines. All of them had to fight their way through clouds of flying spray and sand.

The U.S. 500cc Grand Prix
at Unadilla, New York, attracts
crowds of spectators and many
contestants from Europe who hope
to win some of the big money.

Racer Dick Hocking personalizes the tread pattern of his Goodyear dirt track racing tire. Some racers are so particular, they spend days making alterations on their racing tires.

In the Alligator Enduro, riders tackle the Florida countryside. The course covers everything from swamps to paved roads.

In spite of the fact that they were racing over a wide beach, there were always a few accidents. Some lost control and plowed into others. There were always those who misjudged or took chances. The beach itself had its own hazards. Rocks and logs hidden in the sand were a real danger, and so were holes and soggy patches.

Storms were also a force to be reckoned with. An early tide could sweep over the course and wash away the marker flags. Visibility would be cut to almost nil, and racers could very easily find themselves waist-deep in the English Channel or the Irish Sea.

Sand racing, however, was fun and was considerably less dangerous than some of the other races.

SPEEDWAY RACING

It is generally believed that speedway racing was born at farm fairs in Australia around 1925. The Australians loved the rough-and-tumble sport. Young men with stripped-down, hotted-up motorcycles chased one another around short oval tracks.

It was an exciting and sometimes dangerous sport. There were enough spills and thrills to suit everyone. The Australians enjoyed the spectacle so much, in fact, that the Speedway Royal was built in Sydney in 1926, and crowds of 30,000 people were not uncommon.

The sport found its way to Europe and the United States and caught on immediately. By the early 1930s, speedway racing had become one of the most popular spectator sports in both America and Europe.

ENDUROS

An enduro is not a race; endurance is more important than speed in this kind of competition. The event is run over the worst terrain imaginable.

Those who can't endure simply drop out. An enduro is a real challenge for someone willing to take a lot of punishment. The course may be anywhere from 50 to 150 miles (80 to 240 km) in length, and a rider can get pretty well shaken up during that time.

The object of an enduro is to maintain a specified speed. There are checkpoints all along the way. Riders who check in too early or too late lose points or are disqualified. The name of the game, of course, is to lose as few points as possible.

The winner is not the rider who crosses the finish line first, but the rider who has the best score.

OBSERVED TRIALS COMPETITIONS

Although there is a time limit in observed trials, speed is not the most important factor. Driver control is the heart of this kind of competition. The rider must be mentally alert every inch of the way because even a tiny error could cost him or her points—or even the event itself.

As might be expected, the course covers some brutal terrain. This usually includes sharp turns on steep hillsides, deep sand, slippery banks, muddy gulches, swift streams, and other hazards.

Opposite page: speed doesn't count in observed trials. Part of this contest was to shoot off a ramp and ride on to the next hurdle. *Above:* observed trials are not races. The object is to get from point A to point B without breaking any of the rules laid down by the committee. *Left:* this rider must bounce his way over a pile of tires—and move on to face more obstacles ahead.

Right: the water hazard is tougher than it looks. If the bike drowns out, the cyclist must get it back in running condition—and he'll probably lose valuable points. *Below:* this competitor conquers one of the most challenging obstacles of the course. *Opposite page:* the fact that this driver put his foot down trying not to go over the edge will cost him heavily in points. Feet must stay in position during all observed trials.

Crossing country like this is tough enough. The rules, however, make the competition even tougher. Points are lost if a competitor fails to keep moving forward. There are penalties for touching the ground with a foot, and more points are lost if a rider leaves the marked boundary of a section.

MOTOCROSS   This type of motorcycling competition was born in Europe. It was introduced to the United States in the 1960s. Since that time, it has become the most popular motorcycling participant sport in America.

Any qualified biker between the ages of six and sixty can enter a competition. The events, of course, are geared to the age level. A six-year-old on a bike with a piston displacement of only 50 cubic centimeters (cc) wouldn't be pitted against a twenty-year-old on a powerful 500cc machine.

A motocross rider who really takes racing seriously has to be in superb physical condition. His or her body takes a beating during a race. Up in the air as much as on the ground, the driver has no time at all to relax.

Opposite page: a biker battles his way around the "Snake Pit" in a motocross competition. Motocross was born in Europe and came to America in the 1970s. *Left:* motocross competitions aren't for amateurs. A jump like this requires a great deal of skill and perfect balance.

Bumps, jumps, steep hills, water crossings, and sharp turns keep the rider alert. No matter how alert the riders are, though, spills and other mishaps are common sights during every competition.

And that's why motocross brings out the crowds. People love excitement—and that's one thing that they're all guaranteed to see at a motocross.

CROSS-COUNTRY SCRAMBLES

Cross-country scrambles are popular events, but they're not really in the same league with observed trials competitions, motocrosses, or enduros. No big money is involved, and no big names are on the scene. Moreover, spectators see very little of the action.

The typical cross-country scrambler is someone who simply loves taking his or her bike off into the bush. Ten, twenty, or thirty more enthusiasts are enough to organize a scramble.

A scramble is a point-to-point cross-country race. It usually begins at one location and ends at another. The course is entirely off-road, but a rugged track or trail may link the starting and finishing stations. The trail is often hard to follow, so the organizers mark it with a series of cardboard arrows.

Opposite page: a slight miscalculation could cause a cyclist to wind up in the bottom of the pit. *Left:* "Magic" Mark Barnett, 125cc National Motocross Champion, is one of the most famous motorcycle racers in America. *Below:* Darrell Schultz takes one last jump as an official swings the checkered flag and declares him the winner of this motocross competition.

The rules of a cross-country scramble couldn't be more simple. It's an all-out race and a mighty aggressive one at that. There's only one winner and that's the rider who covers the total distance in the shortest time.

ROAD RACING AND JUST ABOUT EVERYTHING ELSE

Daytona Beach, Florida, is America's motorcycling super spectacular. For one week in March, the town virtually belongs to the motorcyclists. There are tens of thousands of them and they come from everywhere. Some have come to race; most have come merely to have a good time.

The professionals take Daytona very seriously. There is big money to be won, and with a bit of luck an unknown rider can suddenly become famous. Just about every big name in motorcycling can be seen in Daytona in March, and virtually every type of racing spectacular takes place.

Road racing on Daytona's supertrack is only for the experts. The amateurs belong in the bleachers. The track is a tricky, high-speed oval.

It consists of narrow, winding roadways that suddenly become multilane speedways. A cyclist will top 160 miles (256 km) per hour on the straightaway, then suddenly be driving in little more than an alley. It takes only a tiny error in judgment to be out of the running until the following March.

TRAIL BIKES

There are several million motorcycles that are seldom seen on the road. They are known as trail bikes and are used in the most unlikely places. In some respects, they have taken the place of our old friend the horse.

Cowboys in the West use motorcycles to herd cattle. Forest rangers use them on patrol. Many of the Royal Canadian Mounted Police are now mounted on motorcycles. Telephone and telegraph linespeople use them in areas that once could only be reached on horseback. Miners, explorers, archaeologists, prospectors, trappers, lumberjacks, and any number of other outdoorspeople have found that trail bikes are an excellent means of transportation.

The biggest buyers of trail bikes are people who simply want to get away from it all. They may like to hunt or fish, or they may simply love living next to nature. Their bikes will take them into remote, unspoiled areas, and that's where they're happiest. They prefer the silence of the forests, deserts, and mountains to the noisy confusion of the city.

Fortunately, America still has tremendous tracts of beautiful wilderness area. Until quite recently, many places could be reached only by hikers and on horseback.

These areas are now accessible to the trail bikers. They love the great outdoors and do their best to keep it clean and beautiful for others.

The Daytona
International Speedway.
Both cars and motorcycles
are raced here.

Right: in the early days of Daytona racing, crowds came to watch the races even though there were no stands. *Below:* Race Week comes to Daytona Beach every March. Bikers come from all over the United States, but only a fraction of them enter the races. *Opposite page:* the Motorcycle Parade is one of the few organized events besides the races themselves. Here the bikers parade across Silver Beach Bridge.

Opposite page: sitting in a motorcycle sidecar, watching the crowds . . . *Left:* bikers at Daytona take the races seriously—but everything else is fun and games. *Below:* bikes of every kind are seen at Daytona during Race Week.

The superbikes—street bikes that have
been modified for racing—are off.
The slower bikes take off seconds later.

Number 99 couldn't make it
around this turn . . .

This biker raises hay as he
smashes through a barrier.

Another racer later managed to
untangle himself from his bike
and get back into the running.

**Number 152 takes a fall in
a Production Bike Heat Race.**

Top: the hay threw Number 41 out of control. He bounced back onto the track and lost his bike.
Below: this rider has to cross the pole successfully before he can continue the competition.

A spectacular jump at
a motocross competition
at Daytona.

Top: the start of the first lap
of the 1981 Daytona 200. *Bottom:*
Dale Singleton races past the crowd.

Opposite page: Dale Singleton, winner of the 1981 Daytona 200, holds his trophy high while his friend holds mascot Elmer the Third. Dale says that Elmer brings him luck. *Left:* Kenny Roberts, who has won the 500cc World Racing Championship three times, often competes at Daytona.

Above: Gina Bovaird, a highly skilled cyclist, has raced at Daytona and at international meetings in Europe. *Right:* Daytona racer Carter Alsop.

7 LITTLE MACHINES AND LITTLE PEOPLE

SCOOTERS The Autoped Company of New York came out with its first scooter in 1915. The scooter offered certain advantages, it's true, but it also had more than its share of disadvantages. Perhaps its worst feature was the fact that it had no seat. The rider had to stand up and hang on for dear life. The Autoped could easily hit 35 miles (56 km) per hour. Anyone who fell off at that speed, of course, was almost certain to sustain serious injuries.

In spite of their shortcomings, scooters became quite popular with women. The rear wheel and drive belt were covered so that there was no danger of skirts or petticoats becoming entangled in the works. Manufacturers designed scooters in bright colors to attract women customers. They even equipped them with solid rubber tires so that women would not have any tire problems.

The Scootamota, the Unibus, and the two-seater Reynolds Runabout were the most popular makes in the 1920s. They were simple and economical to run and easy to maintain. Women had no trouble handling them, and the fact that most scooters now had seats added greatly to their appeal.

Unfortunately, scooters never caught on in a big way in the United States. They became more and more popular in Europe and South East Asia, but they simply could not compete with the growing popularity of minibikes and motorcycles in the United States. Competition from small cars also helped to force the unfortunate scooter off the road.

MOPEDS It was probably the bleak economic picture of 1975 that kicked off the moped boom in the United States. The price of gas kept getting higher and higher, and the second car in the garage no longer seemed to be such a good idea. After all, there was a big difference between 15 miles (24 km) to a gallon (4 l) and well over 100 miles (160 m) to a gallon.

Anyone who thinks that mopeds are strictly for the younger generation is dead wrong. A survey by *Popular Mechanics* magazine revealed that mopeds appeal to all age groups. Students drive them to school, and grandmothers drive them to the supermarket. In praise of her moped, a 74-year-old Michigan woman said, "Oh, I simply love it! I really do!"

A Florida high school student said, "It's the ideal thing for around here because there are never any parking problems. I can be in class or in study hall while kids in cars are still trying to find a place to park."

Tens of thousands of people commute to work on their mopeds. The average round trip for a commuter seems to be about 12 or 13 miles (19 or 20 km). An Indianapolis secretary, however, averages 70 miles (112 km) a day driving to and from work. "I use my car only when I absolutely have to," she stated.

Many others feel the same way. The American dream of two cars in every garage no longer seems possible. Now it seems to be one small car and a moped or motorcycle or two in every garage.

PRIZES FOR ALMOST EVERYONE

How old do you have to be to enter a motorcycle race? The answer may come as a bit of a surprise. Children no more than two and a half years old compete on tracks all over the country. What's more, they take their racing very seriously.

They can hardly be blamed. Many of the entrants are awarded trophies. They're worth only a couple of dollars at the very most, but they mean the world to those who win them.

As a matter of fact, parents often want the trophies just as much as the children do. It makes parents very proud to boast that their three-, four-, or five-year-old son or daughter won a trophy in a motorcycle race.

Just about any child on a pair of motor-driven wheels can enter a race. Entrance fees vary from two dollars to ten dollars.

At all tracks, races are divided into age groups. There are events for the two and a half- to six-year-olds and events for those of seven and eight. The nine- to eleven-year-olds have their own races as do the twelve- through sixteen-year-olds. The seventeen-year-olds have outgrown the smaller machines and are ready to go on to bigger vehicles.

The winner in every class gets a trophy. Those who come in second, third, fourth, or even fifth often get one as well. Trophies are so important that there are some races in which every entry gets one. All a child has to do to win a prize is to show up at the starting line. Some children may fall off before even getting started, but they get a trophy just the same.

Although children generally love racing, it can sometimes be rather hard on the parents. It's not easy to watch your preschool-age child tearing around a racetrack on a motorcycle at 45 miles (72 km) per hour.

Another hardship for parents is the expense. Even a tiny bike for a three-year-old costs several hundred dollars. Boots, helmets, and other necessary protection cost a couple of hundred more. The mechanic's bills are another expensive item, and they can't be avoided.

Opposite page, top: this Master Index Scootamota of 1919 was popular in England. *Opposite page, bottom:* the Lambretta Electronic starts easily and is noted for reliability. *Left:* although this Vespa resembles a scooter, the law in England classifies it as a moped and a car license is needed to drive it. *Below:* the Vespa Ciao moped is particularly popular in Europe.

Above: the Honda PA50 moped. *Right:* this cyclist wanted to attract attention . . .

Above: many manufacturers produce models especially for children. *Right:* a lesson on safety before she goes riding off. . .

This, of course, is only the beginning. Children outgrow their bikes and equipment almost overnight. Their boots and helmets are suddenly too small, and the bikes aren't fast enough. And this isn't something that happens only once, but time after time. About the only item that doesn't have to be replaced every year is the van or camper that carries the bike out to the track.

In spite of the expense, more youngsters than ever are racing motorcycles. One writer puts the number at approximately 25,000 and says that there are about 2,000 tracks in the United States. The little bike racers are becoming big business. In fact, they even have their own magazine, called *Bicycle Moto-Cross News (BMX)*.

But isn't motorcycle racing a dangerous sport? Yes, it can be. So children are taught safety first. Their parents stress safety, and so do the adult officials at the tracks. Speed is fine, but reckless or careless riding is not allowed. Racing is racing, though, and there are always spills, thrills, and chills. Major injuries are rare, however, and the child who is frightened out on the tracks is even rarer.

Right: a young Imp shoots off a ramp and over a number of his friends and a car. *Opposite page:* a poster promoting the Imps Motor Cycle Display Team. The Imps' fame has spread throughout the United Kingdom, the United States, and Europe.

IMPS Motor Cycle Display Team

THE HACKNEY IMPS

The boys in the London suburb of Hackney, England, consider themselves very fortunate. They have a hero and his name is Roy Pratt. Pratt is a big, strapping London police officer, and boys are his special interest.

It wouldn't be fair to say that the boys in Hackney were any more of a problem than boys anywhere else. They roamed the streets in their spare time, and a few of them sometimes got into mischief. It was seldom anything serious, but Officer Pratt knew that minor incidents often lead to something more serious.

The police officer talked to some of the parents and they listened. None of them liked the idea of their sons roaming aimlessly through the streets of the city. They wanted to keep the boys in their own neighborhood, and Roy Pratt thought he knew how this could be done. It would cost the parents some money, but it would be spent on a good cause.

Pratt planned to organize a motorcycle display team. Any boy between the ages of six and fifteen was eligible to try out. There were almost no motorcycles in the beginning, but most parents seemed willing to buy one if their sons showed promise.

The Hackney Adventure Project, as it was called, was an immediate success. The initial shortage of motorcycles did very little to dampen the boys' enthusiasm. Pratt and the fathers taught them how to ride, constantly stressing the importance of safety. The boys loved the experience and proudly referred to themselves as the Imps.

Much to everyone's delight, motorcycles kept popping up at a surprising rate. Proud parents wanted to buy bikes for their sons. Community fund-raising groups raised enough money for a couple of bikes. A few more were donated by local merchants. Officer Pratt persuaded his fellow police officers to donate enough money for two minicycles. An enterprising father convinced two motorcycle distributors that it would be excellent publicity to donate a bike each to the Hackney Adventure group.

Pratt's pupils were wildly enthusiastic. Although most of them had never been on a motorcycle before, they eagerly looked forward to the experience. This pleased Pratt. The police officer wanted a motorcycle display team, and he was determined to have a good one.

The Imps learned quickly. Pratt trained them as precision riders, and he trained them well. Today the young riders can perform most of the tricks of stunt riders. The younger kids shoot off ramps and take flying leaps through circles of fire. Only the older riders are permitted to attempt the high-risk events, however.

Perhaps the pyramid is the group's most spectacular precision stunt. This involves almost the entire team and doesn't allow for any mistakes. One by one, the Imps climb aboard a full-sized motorcycle piloted by Pratt himself. Each Imp assumes a carefully worked out position. Perfect balance is of the utmost importance. If one Imp wobbles too much, the whole team comes tumbling down. It has happened many times, of course, but Pratt is a patient man.

The fame of the Hackney Adventure Project spread rapidly. Pratt and the Imps appeared on television several times. They also put on shows in many places throughout England. Their performances were always well received. Young and old alike were thrilled to see boys from six to fifteen years of age performing like professionals. Their stunts looked extremely dangerous, but their training had been thorough. Their trainer had seen to that.

Officer Pratt must be the busiest police officer in London. When he's not on duty, he's either working with the Imps or answering questions. Town officials from all corners of England come to see him. They have seen the Hackney Adventure Project in action, and they want to know how to form similar groups in their own communities.

They know, too, that since the formation of the Hackney Adventure Project, juvenile delinquency in the London suburb of Hackney has just about become a thing of the past. Doing stunts on a motorcycle is much more exciting than roaming the streets and getting into trouble.

8 SPEED, SAFETY, AND MORE MOTORCYCLES

HOW FAST CAN THEY GO?

On August 5, 1963, Craig Breedlove drove his *Spirit of America* over the Bonneville Salt Flats in Utah at 407.45 miles (651.92 km) per hour. The 400-mile-per-hour (640-km-per-hour) barrier had been smashed at last, and Breedlove was a very happy man.

But he wasn't happy for very long. Race officials decided that Breedlove's car was *not* a car. It had only three wheels; therefore, it was a motorcycle.

But what a motorcycle it was! In fact, it was the only one like it in the world. It was about the size of a jet fighter plane without wings and was powered by a jet airplane engine.

The *Spirit of America* didn't look like a plane or a car, and it certainly didn't look like a motorcycle. Breedlove insisted that his car was a car, but the officials couldn't make up their minds. Over a year passed before the final decision was made. The officials then announced that the *Spirit of America* was not a motorcycle after all. It was a three-wheeled car.

This news came as a bit of a blow to some motorcyclists. They could no longer say that a rider had hit over 400 miles (640 km) per hour on a bike. The present record was now just under half that speed.

Then a man named Donald Vesco came along. On September 28, 1975, Vesco recorded an average speed of 304 miles (486.4 km) per hour over the measured mile (1.6 km) at the Bonneville Salt Flats. This speed established a new American Motorcyclist Association record. Just to prove that he hadn't simply had a stroke of luck, Vesco decided to run through the measured mile one more time. He averaged 303 miles (484.8 km) per hour on his second attempt.

Anyone else would have called it a day, but Vesco still wasn't entirely satisfied. He told officials that he wanted a try at the flying quarter mile (.4 km). The officials agreed, and the young man from El Cajon, California, took a deep breath and got back on his bike.

This time it was the officials who took a deep breath. Their stop watches told them that Vesco had covered the quarter mile in 2.925 seconds. That meant that he had maintained an average speed of 308 miles (492.8 km) per hour for the quarter mile.

Then, in September 1978, he set the world motorcycle land speed record at 318.598 miles (509.756 km) per hour.

Donald Vesco holds the world motorcycle land speed record.

SAFETY FIRST   Just about anyone can be seen on a motorcycle these days. Stop on any corner long enough and you'll most likely see a child on the way to school, someone headed for work, a doctor rushing off to visit a patient, or a traffic officer cruising the streets on a big Harley-Davidson. All of these riders have at least one thing in common: they are all very safety conscious.

Safe riding habits are the most important part of any rider education course. The American Motorcyclist Association constantly stresses safety. In 1979, more than 400 organizations offered motorcycle rider education courses. Although the courses were strictly voluntary, more than 20,000 students attended. Schools and local police also offered courses in hundreds of towns.

Manufacturers want people to know that motorcycling is no more dangerous than walking or bicycling. Safety is stressed everytime they make a sale or instruct a rider.

AND NOW WHAT?   We seem to have entered the Age of Motorcycling in a big way. In 1963, there were less than half a million motorcycles registered in the United States. By 1980, the number topped six million. Actually, there were a couple of million more than that. There were the trail or off-road bikes which did not have to be registered because they were never used on the highways. There are probably about ten million bikes in the United States today.

There are several reasons for the sudden interest in motorcycling. For one thing, the image of the motorcyclist has changed dramatically. The Hell's Angels image has just about disappeared. People now recognize that motorcycling is not something reserved strictly for the young. The American Motorcyclist Association and the manufacturers and distributors have worked hard to give motorcycling a good name. They want people to know that motorcycling is for everyone, and they've worked hard to get this idea across.

The Honda CZ500 Deluxe

Opposite page, top: the Yamaha XS Eleven.
Opposite page, bottom: the Harley-Davidson
XLH Sportster. *Above:* the BMW R65.

Opposite page, top: the Harley-Davidson FLT
Classic Tour Glide. *Opposite page, bottom:*
the Harley Davidson FXB Sturgis Belt Drive.
Above: the Harley-Davidson FXS Low Rider.

There are now bikes to suit just about every size and taste.
Suzuki alone has nearly 50 different models. Kawasaki, Yamaha, and
Honda have very nearly the same number. This gives the customer
hundreds of models from which to choose.

There's a bike for everyone! All of the manufacturers offer little
bikes for little ones and larger bikes for those who want something
big and powerful. Some are designed for trips to the supermarket;
others are strictly for sport.

The single most important reason for motorcycling's growing
popularity is undoubtedly economy. Gasoline is becoming more
expensive. It may cost four or five dollars to take the car on a shop-
ping trip. The same trip could be made for under a dollar by bike.

Many two-car families are now becoming one-car-and-one-
motorcycle families. It makes sound economic sense. If there are
children in the family, there may be several motorcycles in the garage.

There may even be one for Grandma and Grandpa.

BIBLIOGRAPHY

MAGAZINE ARTICLES

Bahr, Robert. "From Crud to Chrome." *Popular Mechanics*, July 1977.

Boyce, Tim. "Riviera Racer." *Which Bike?*, February 1981.

Buzzelli, Buzz. "In the Spirit of Simplicity." *Cycle*, January 1981.

Cameron, Kevin. "A Long Day at Loudon." *Cycle*, October 1979.

Dempewolff, Richard. "Daring Young Bikers." *Popular Mechanics*, August 1977.

Haveman, Ernest. "Down Will Come Baby, Cycle, and All." *Sports Illustrated*, August 1973.

Hawkins, Dave. "Carlsbad Grand Prix." *Cycle*, September 1978.

Jones, Robert. "Make It or Break It." *Sports Illustrated*, September 2, 1974.

Jones, Robert. "We Shoulda' Run One More Test." *Sports Illustrated*, September 16, 1974.

Leven, Dan. "High Jumping to a Conclusion." *Sports Illustrated*, November 19, 1973.

Martin, Terry. "A Harley for the Pioneer." *Classic Bike*, March 1981.

Reese, Rex. "A Short History of Stadium Motocross." *Motocross*, April 1981.

Reese, Rex. "The Inner Game of Motocross." *Pro Riding Secrets*, March 1981.

Self, Charles. "Long Way from Popping Wheelies." *Popular Mechanics*, January 1974.

Stermer, Bill. "Harley-Davidson at 75: Alive and Thriving." *Cycle*, October 1978.

Weisel, Jody. "Trans-USA Championship." *Motocross Action*, February 1981.

BOOKS

Arctander, Eric. *The Book of Motorcycles, Trail Bikes & Scooters*. New York: Arco, 1965.

Engel, Lyle Kenyon. *The Complete Book of Minibikes and Minicycles*. New York: Arco, 1976.

Griffin, Al. *Motorcycles*. Chicago: Henry Regnery, 1972.

Olney, Ross R. *Motorcycling*. New York: Franklin Watts, 1975.

Partridge, Michael. *Motorcycle Pioneers: The Men, the Machines, the Events: 1860–1930*. New York: Arco, 1977.

Radlauer, Ed. *Motorcyclopedia*. Glendale, California: Bowman, 1976.

Radlauer, Ed and Dan. *Motorcycle Moto Cross School*. New York: Franklin Watts, 1975.

Redman, Martin. *Superbike*. New York: Harper and Row, 1975.

Reid, Peter. *The Motorcycle Book*. Garden City, New York: Doubleday, 1967.

Seever, R. *Mopeds*. New York: Harvery House, 1979.

Terry, Arthur. *The Moped Handbook*. New York: Crown, 1977.

Tragatch, Erwin. *The Complete Illustrated Encyclopedia of the World's Motorcycles*. New York: Holt, Rinehart, and Winston, 1977.

INDEX